Interim NWCG Minimum Standards for Medical Units Managed By NWCG Member Agencies

NWCG Safety and Health Working Team
Incident Emergency Medical Task Group

Revised on September 7, 2010

To: NWCG Member Agencies, GACCs, IMTs and Medical Unit Leaders

This document was amended by the Risk Management Committee (RMC), formerly known as the Safety and Health Working Team (SHWT), on September 7, 2010. The only change to the document is the one listed below on this page:

"The Interim NWCG Minimum Standards for Medical Units is designed to be utilized as a baseline or minimum expectations for EMS personnel and services associated with Federal wildland fire incidents."

Was changed to:

"The Interim NWCG Minimum Standards for Medical Units is designed to be utilized as a baseline or minimum expectations for EMS personnel and services associated with wildland fire incidents managed by NWCG member agencies."

The document will now read (correction is highlighted):

After years of hard work and effort put forth by representatives from NWCG member agencies, the National Association of EMS Officials (NASEMSO), the National Association of EMS Physicians (NAEMSP), numerous outside organizations, and from individual medical unit leaders The Interim NWCG *Minimum Standards for Medical Units has been published.* This document reflects a national approach focused on providing a coordinated, uniformed, and comprehensive delivery of emergency medical services (EMS) and occupational health on Federal wildland fires in the United States of America. **The *Interim NWCG Minimum Standards for Medical Units* is designed to be utilized as a baseline or minimum expectations for EMS personnel and services associated with wildland fire incidents managed by NWCG member agencies.** However, medical directors of various programs and agencies may identify alternative standards for use within their jurisdictional purview, therefore if questions or discrepancies are found, consult the appropriate medical director or state EMS authority.

Annually or when deemed appropriate, the NWCG will update the Interim NWCG *Minimum Standards for Medical Units* procedures, guidelines, supplies and equipment identified within this document. Any changes shall be channeled through the NWCG and posted on the Safety and Health Working Team (SHWT) Incident Emergency Medical Task Group's (IEMTG) web page located at:

www.nwcg.gov/teams/shwt/iemtg/index.html

Due to continual updating of the document, for those utilizing a hard copy, it is strongly recommended to ensure it is the latest version by referencing the IEMTG website listed above.

Table of Contents

Appendices

Revised on September 7, 2010

Definitions

Advanced EMT (AEMT) – An Emergency Medical Services (EMS) professional who provides basic and limited advanced life support skills and interventions for patients within an EMS system.

Advanced Life Support (ALS) – Emergency medical care and interventions performed by an Advanced Emergency Medical Technician (EMT) or Paramedic with limited supervision, using critical thinking and autonomous decision making skills which includes invasive procedures and medication administration.

Basic Life Support (BLS) – Emergency medical care and interventions performed by an Emergency Medical Technician (EMT) with minimal equipment, limited medications and non-invasive procedures.

Certification – The issuing of certificates by an agency based upon standards adopted by that agency that are usually based upon minimum competence. Competency certification does not constitute permission to practice.

Emergency Medical System– A network of services coordinated to provide aid and medical assistance from primary response to definitive care, involving personnel trained in the rescue, stabilization, transportation, and advanced treatment of traumatic or medical emergencies. Linked by a communication system that operates on both a local and a regional level, EMS is a tiered system of care, which is usually initiated by citizen action in the form of a telephone call to an emergency number. Subsequent stages include the emergency medical dispatch, first medical responder, ambulance personnel, medium and heavy rescue equipment, and paramedic units, if necessary. In the hospital, service is provided by emergency department nurses, emergency department physicians, specialists, and critical care nurses and physicians.

Emergency Medical Technician (EMT) – An EMS professional who provides basic life support skills and interventions for patients within an EMS system.

Expanded Role – Skills and interventions not included in the *National EMS Scope of Practice Model* necessary for EMS professionals functioning in health care settings other than the typical prehospital setting including, but not limited to, wildland fire medical units.

Incident Command System (ICS) – A combination of facilities, equipment, personnel, procedures and communications operating within a common organizational structure, with responsibility for the management of assigned resources to effectively accomplish stated objectives pertaining to an incident.

Licensed Physician – A physician licensed by or exempted from licensure by a state Board of Medicine to practice medicine or surgery in that state.

Revised on September 7, 2010

Licensure – The act of a State granting an entity permission to do something that the entity could not legally do without such permission. Licensing is generally viewed by legislative bodies as a regulatory effort to protect the public from potential harm. A license is generally considered a privilege and not a right.

Medical Advisor – A physician or other health care professional used as a subject matter expert.

Medical Director – A physician responsible for the overall medical care provided in the field.

Medical Kit – The generic term applying to NFES 1760, NFES 1835 and/or the sub-kits associated with NFES 1835.

Medical Unit – The ICS unit that is responsible for the emergency medical and occupational health care of incident personnel.

Medical Unit Leader(MEDL) – The ICS position responsible for supervising the Medical Unit and assigned Medical Unit personnel.

Medical Unit Personnel – Personnel assigned to function under the direction of the Medical Unit Leader.

National Association of State EMS Officials (NASEMSO) – The lead organization for developing national EMS policy and oversight, providing vision, leadership and resources for the improvement of state, regional and local EMS and emergency care systems.

National EMS Scope of Practice Model – The *National EMS Scope of Practice Model* published by the National Highway Traffic Safety Administration defines and describes four EMS licensure levels: Emergency Medical Responder (EMR), Emergency Medical Technician (EMT), Advanced EMT (AEMT), and Paramedic. Each level represents a unique role, set of skills, and knowledge base.

National Registry of Emergency Medical Technicians (NREMT) – An organization that ensures graduates of EMS educational programs have met minimal standards by measuring competency through a uniform testing process.

On-Line Medical Direction – The physician or designee on the radio or phone who gives real time medical direction to the out-of-hospital providers.

Over-the-Counter (OTC) Medications – Drugs that can be purchased without a prescription.

Paramedic – An EMS professional who provides basic and advanced life support skills and interventions for patients within an EMS system.

Revised on September 7, 2010

Scope of Practice – A predefined set of skills, interventions or other activities that an EMS professional is legally authorized to perform when necessary, usually set by state law or regulation and local medical direction.

Standard of Care – Conduct exercising the degree of care, skill, and judgment that would be expected under like or similar circumstances by a similarly educated, reasonable EMS professional.

Revised on September 7, 2010

Executive Summary

This document introduces stakeholders to the minimum standards developed by the Incident Emergency Medical Task Group (IEMTG) when a Medical Unit has been established by a National Wildfire Coordinating Group (NWCG) member agency. This document is intended to provide direction regarding medical personnel and equipment assigned to the Medical Unit.

The IEMTG recognizes the *National EMS Scope of Practice Model* as the baseline standard for emergency medical service providers. Therefore, a key component of the minimum standards addresses the recognition of local, state, federal, and tribal jurisdictional authorities and the integration of medical services. Overall, the minimum standards seek to ensure that incident personnel receive quality, timely medical care on wildland fire incidents, which often occur in remote areas.

These minimum standards support the following goals of the IEMTG:

- Facilitate the national mobility and availability of EMS personnel for wildland fire incidents.
- Establish a scope of practice and promote a standard of care for medical personnel assigned to a Medical Unit on a wildland fire incident.
- Provide national wildland fire emergency medical and occupational health standards to ensure the health and safety of incident personnel in an efficient and cost effective manner on wildland fire incidents.
- Minimize negative impact on local emergency medical service resources, clinics and hospitals.
- Identify skills and medications needed on wildland fire incidents.
- Provide guidelines for appropriate emergency medical service personnel and equipment to properly staff incidents.

The IEMTG will continue efforts to address companion documents for other components of medical operations for wildland fire incidents to include, but not limited to:

- Development of NWCG Wildland Fire EMS Protocols.
- Additional training needed by Medical Unit Leaders and EMS personnel on wildland fire incidents.
- Establish standardized data collection terminology and minimum data set to be collected for patients on NWCG incidents.

Introduction

The care of the sick and injured on wildland fire incidents has expanded over the last 30 years. The mission of Medical Units on wildland fire incidents has evolved into a complex service which provides: (1) stabilization and emergency medical treatment of incident personnel, and (2) occupational health and preventative measures for incident personnel to remain safe and healthy.

Wildland firefighting operations require a unique array of services due to the remoteness, terrain, and complexity of utilizing multiple agencies. Medical support is essential because of the inherent risks and exposures associated with these events. The issues of standard of care and legal licensure of providers come into play when emergency medical providers from other jurisdictions cross state lines or other geopolitical boundaries to provide medical care.

These situations are further complicated in areas where medical control is sometimes nonexistent or the capabilities of nearby medical facilities may be limited, including the variability of local emergency medical services agency capacities.

The NWCG is comprised of nine agencies.

- Bureau of Land Management
- Bureau of Indian Affairs
- U.S. Fish and Wildlife
- National Park Service
- U.S. Forest Service, Fire and Aviation Management
- Fire Systems Research, U.S. Forest Service
- National Association of State Foresters
- U.S. Fire Administration
- Intertribal Timber Council

The NWCG Safety and Health Working Team (SHWT) formed and chartered the IEMTG to address the issues of medical care on NWCG managed incidents.

The IEMTG is comprised of members from:

- Bureau of Land Management
- Bureau of Indian Affairs
- National Park Service
- U.S. Forest Service
- National Association of State Foresters
- National Association of State EMS Officials

Background

NWCG member agencies recognize a difference between the typical 911/prehospital short-term patient contacts versus the unique healthcare needs of wildland fire personnel. A common role of EMS providers is to care for patients briefly at the request of a 911 EMS system. On wildland fire incidents, EMS providers may also serve to monitor and detect when minor illnesses or injuries require referral to definitive care.

Federal, state, tribal, and local wildland fire agencies and their personnel continue to lack clearly defined standards and protocols to follow in the practice of emergency medical services (EMS) on incidents. This situation has led to a lack of uniform and consistent standards between multiple agencies and state EMS organizations.

The IEMTG conducted a gap analysis comparing the *National EMS Scope of Practice Model* with the existing medical programs of NWCG members already being utilized on wildland fire incidents. Included in this gap analysis were the National Park Service, Alaska Fire Medic Program, Cal Fire, Smokejumper Programs and the Incident Medical Specialist Programs. The results revealed considerable variation and validated the need for incident medical standards specific to wildland fire Medical Units.

Medical Scope of Practice

A scope of practice in a medical profession is a description of what a state licensed individual legally can and cannot do. States vary by what medical interventions, devices, and medications (referred to in this document as "skills") are permitted for each level of EMS provider. The *National EMS Scope of Practice Model* identifies the minimum psychomotor skills, interventions and knowledge base necessary for entry level competence of each nationally identified level of EMS provider. The following link can be used to view the *National EMS Scope of Practice Model* www.EMS.gov. Appendix A contains a synopsis of the skills allowed, by level, in the *National EMS Scope of Practice Model*.

Under this model, to be eligible for state licensure, EMS personnel must be verifiably competent in the minimum knowledge and skills needed to ensure safe and effective practice at that level. This competence is assured by the successful completion of an EMS educational program and written and practical certification exams. A state EMS license for an individual EMS provider issued by one state is the basis of the ability for another state to legally recognize that provider while they are functioning in the other state.

NWCG recognizes the *National EMS Scope of Practice Model* as the baseline standard for incident emergency medical service providers assigned to a Medical Unit. These Medical Units utilize three of the EMS provider levels identified in the *National EMS Scope of Practice Model* which are the Emergency Medical Technician (EMT), Advanced EMT (AEMT), and Paramedic.

The NWCG agencies have a moral, ethical and legal obligation to provide appropriate medical care for incident personnel. Due to the remote and hazardous nature of wildland fire incidents, Medical Units must be staffed by qualified medical personnel trained to function in this unique environment. A benefit of a properly staffed wildland fire Medical Unit includes being as self sufficient as possible with a reduced negative impact to local emergency medical services, clinics, and hospitals. Additionally, a cost savings to local, state, tribal and federal incident funding agencies is achieved by limiting off-site medical expenses for minor illnesses and injuries of incident personnel. Ultimately, wildfire EMS personnel help to keep incident personnel operational and available for their mission.

Two different categories of medically related tasks are important considerations at any wildland fire Medical Unit. The first is the role of the Medical Unit to make commonly available over-the-counter (OTC) medications and supplies available to incident personnel in a manner that correlates to what would be available in a community. The second is a process of determining the availability, medical necessity, and legality of skills which may differ from those defined in the *National EMS Scope of Practice Model*.

Commonly Available Medications, Interventions and Supplies

Incident medical personnel with appropriate training and medical direction may be authorized to make available limited quantities of OTC medications supplied in the National Fire Equipment System (NFES) medical kits and basic supplies such as bandages or other materials. Other OTC medications specific to the needs of the incident may be ordered by the Medical Unit Leader (MEDL) with approval by medical direction.

It is important to note that the Medical Unit personnel are not "diagnosing" a condition and determining which and what quantity of the OTCs should be ingested or applied by the incident personnel visiting the Medical Unit. Activities of the Medical Unit personnel include monitoring and maintaining the supply of OTCs. This may involve reading product names or labels to individuals with English reading literacy problems or observing and documenting patterns of use that may warrant reporting. An example is a sudden increase in the number and frequency of Medical Unit personnel visits requesting an anti-diarrheal for self administration.

Medical Unit personnel may also make recommendations and assist with simple interventions that are not regulated as part of any EMS provider's scope of practice, and are commonly administered at home or among co-workers in other settings. Examples include: taking a temperature, applying a bandage, or assisting an individual with something they cannot reach or do for themselves such as applying an OTC anti-itch lotion to the back of an individual with poison oak.

Revised on September 7, 2010

NWCG Wildland Fire Scope of Practice

NWCG member agency Medical Units have historically provided some interventions not commonly used in prehospital EMS such as superficial wound and blister care and eye wash for incident personnel. Uncommon interventions provided by Medical Unit EMS personnel may be necessary due to wildland fire specific hazards, the remote nature or delayed transport times for injured or ill personnel. If not contained within the *National EMS Scope of Practice Model*, additional interventions may only be performed if three specific criteria are met. These conditions must be verified and documented before Medical Unit EMS personnel may provide the additional skills.

The scope of practice for EMS personnel assigned to a Medical Unit will conform to the skills and devices in the current *National EMS Scope of Practice Model* for the level at which they were assigned and are functioning, unless these three conditions are met:

1. The skill(s) must be within the scope of practice of the EMS provider in their state of origin, and
2. The medical director of the Medical Unit must approve the use of the skill(s), and
3. Use of the skill(s) by that level of EMS provider in the state in which the Medical Unit is based must be legal.

Personnel Credentials

The provider of emergency medical care at an NWCG wildland fire Medical Unit will provide a current licensure card from their state EMS licensing agency to the MEDL. The IEMTG recommends that incident EMS personnel carry their EMS licensure card(s) with them. A National Registry of EMTs (NREMT) card is not recognized as a credential which would allow the holder to provide EMS patient care.

The MEDL will complete and submit a "*NWCG Limited Request for Recognition*" (Appendix B) form for each incident to the appropriate EMS state authority for notification of the establishment of a Medical Unit and to validate the EMS licensure of personnel assigned to the Medical Unit. Licenses should be current and unrestricted by the state of origin. The MEDL will verify that each EMS provider (agency and contract) assigned to a Medical Unit has a current state license card from their state EMS licensing agency at or above the level requested.

Revised on September 7, 2010

State EMS Authority Notification

The MEDL will contact the state regulatory agency in charge of EMS within 24 hours and advise them of the establishment of a Medical Unit with the following information:

- Location and contact information of the Medical Unit and MEDL.
- Names of EMS providers present.
- Level of care provided.

The MEDL will ensure a *"Limited Request for Recognition"* form is completed identifying all EMS providers assigned to the Medical Unit. This form will then be submitted to the appropriate state EMS office for the incident. The MEDL will update this information as new EMS personnel arrive or are reassigned or the incident is relocated. The original forms will be retained with the incident Medical Unit records.

If EMS care is provided on a managed incident crossing borders into more than one state, each state regulatory agency in charge of EMS must be notified.

Medical Direction

The Medical Unit medical director is the physician with the overall responsibility for the medical aspects of care provided by the Medical Unit's medical providers at a wildland fire incident. This includes but is not limited to educational activities, patient care review, incident visits and on-line access to the medical director by the Medical Unit's medical providers during an incident for advice and guidance on medical issues.

The local on-line medical director is the physician or designee at the local receiving facility on the radio or phone who gives real time medical direction to the Medical Unit's medical providers during scene care or in transport to the local receiving facility.

Upon establishment of a Medical Unit, the MEDL will make contact with the potential local receiving facilities to include clinic(s), hospital(s) and tertiary care and specialty referral center(s), e.g., trauma or burn center. Contact should determine availability and limitations and define route for on-line medical direction. This should be documented in the Unit Log (ICS-214) and entered into the Medical Plan (ICS-206).

The MEDL will ensure that each EMS provider assigned to the Medical Unit has access to and is familiar with the Medical Unit protocols.

Revised on September 7, 2010

Communications

The Medical Unit will have the ability to maintain contact with unit personnel. The MEDL will work with the communication unit leader to assure that unit personnel receive appropriate communication equipment and training and understand incident communication protocols.

The Medical Unit will establish and maintain communication capabilities for contacting appropriate medical facilities and medical direction. Radio frequency information should be exchanged with the local EMS ground ambulance and air medical transport services and/or the emergency dispatch center. These contacts should be identified on the Medical Plan (ICS-206). Cell or satellite phone technology may be acceptable forms of communications, per incident protocol.

Incident Patient Transportation

The MEDL will notify local/regional EMS transportation resources that an NWCG wildland fire incident is operating within their response area. The patient transport service utilized, whether ground or air, must be a state licensed EMS agency. In some cases, the response areas of available EMS may be crossing state lines, as allowed by multi-agency licensure or interstate compact. The MEDL will post the pre-identified available ground and air transportation options on the Medical Plan (ICS-206).

Air service resources should include information on landing zone options and requirements and back country hoist capabilities. State EMS offices can provide the names and contact information for licensed air medical services.

In some cases, it may be necessary to move a patient by incident air or ground resources to a location accessible by a licensed EMS. The decision to use non-EMS aircraft and vehicles for emergency transport to definitive care is best made in conjunction with medical direction and the receiving facility.

Equipment and Supplies

The National Interagency Support Cache System has established a protocol for ordering and deploying medical kits, which addresses legal requirements and Federal accountability standards.

The cache system does not always have medical kits available for incidents. A reference for recommended non-cache medical equipment and supplies can be found in Appendix C, "Recommended Equipment and Supply List". These lists define the typical equipment and supplies used by the EMT, AEMT and Paramedic EMS provider levels. A list of OTC medications commonly available through Medical Units is also provided. However, these lists are not all inclusive.

Revised on September 7, 2010

The MEDLs can request additional equipment and supplies as allowed by the associated scope of practice of the incident Medical Unit personnel as approved by the incident medical director.

Implementation of Minimum Standards for Medical Units

Initial efforts to validate the status of licensed EMS personnel and standardize medical care on wildland fire incidents resulted in the NWCG developing a *NWCG Limited Request for Recognition* form and a recommended guideline for the establishment of a Medical Unit.

While these documents have already been used voluntarily for years in some states, the *Minimum Standards for Medical Units Managed by NWCG Member Agencies* proposes a comprehensive national standard and unified approach for managing a Medical Unit on wildland fire incidents.

The *Minimum Standards for Medical Units Managed by NWCG Member Agencies* replaces and supersedes the *NWCG Medical Unit Operating Standards for Integration with State EMS*.

A scope of practice does not define a standard of care, nor does it define what should be done in a given situation (i.e., it is not a practice guideline or protocol). A scope of practice defines what is legally permitted to be done by some or all of the licensed individuals at that level, not what must be done.

Following the adoption of the *Minimum Standards for Medical Units Managed by NWCG Member Agencies*, the IEMTG will develop *NWCG Wildland Fire EMS Protocols*.

Revised on September 7, 2010

Appendix A - National EMS Scope of Practice Model Skill Synopsis

The NWCG recognizes the National EMS Scope of Practice Model with each associated skill set, by level. These and any additional skills may only be used by NWCG personnel assigned to a Medical Unit when:
1) The skill(s) is within the scope of practice of the EMS provider in their state of origin, and
2) The medical director of the Medical Unit has approved the use of the skill(s), and
3) The skill(s) is legal by that level of EMS provider in the state where the NWCG Medical Unit is based.

Skill – Airway/Ventilation/Oxygenation	EMT	AEMT	Paramedic
Airway – esophageal		X	X
Airway – supraglottic		X	X
Airway – nasal	X	X	X
Airway – oral	X	X	X
Bag-valve-mask (BVM)	X	X	X
BiPAP/CPAP			X
Chest decompression – needle			X
Chest tube placement – assist only			X
Chest tube – monitoring and management			X
Cricoid pressure (Sellick's Maneuver)	X	X	X
Cricothyrotomy – needle			X
Cricothyrotomy – percutaneous			X
Demand valve – manually triggered ventilation	X	X	X
End tidal CO_2 monitoring/capnography			X
Gastric decompression – NG Tube			X
Gastric decompression – OG Tube			X
Head tilt – chin lift	X	X	X
Intubation – nasotracheal			X
Intubation – orotracheal			X
Jaw-thrust	X	X	X
Jaw-thrust – Modified (trauma)	X	X	X
Mouth-to-barrier	X	X	X
Mouth-to-mask	X	X	X
Mouth-to-mouth	X	X	X
Mouth-to-nose	X	X	X
Mouth-to-stoma	X	X	X
Obstruction – direct laryngoscopy			X
Obstruction – Manual	X	X	X
Oxygen therapy – Humidifiers	X	X	X
Oxygen therapy – Nasal cannula	X	X	X
Oxygen therapy – Non-rebreather mask	X	X	X
Oxygen therapy – partial rebreather mask	X	X	X
Oxygen therapy – simple face mask	X	X	X
Oxygen therapy – Venturi mask	X	X	X
PEEP – therapeutic			X
Pulse oximetry	X	X	X
Suctioning – Upper airway	X	X	X
Suctioning – tracheobronchial		AI	X
Ventilator – Automated transport (ATV)	X	X	X

Revised on September 7, 2010

Skill – Cardiovascular/Circulation	EMT	AEMT	Paramedic
Cardiac monitoring – multi-lead (interpretive)			X
Cardiac monitoring – single lead (interpretive)			X
Cardiopulmonary resuscitation (CPR)	X	X	X
Cardioversion – electrical			X
Carotid massage			X
Defibrillation – automated / semi-automated	X	X	X
Hemorrhage control – direct pressure	X	X	X
Hemorrhage control – tourniquet	X	X	X
Internal; cardiac pacing – monitoring only			X
MAST/PASG	X	X	X
Mechanical CPR device	A	A	A
Transcutaneous pacing – manual			X
Skill – Immobilization	EMT	AEMT	Paramedic
Spinal immobilization – cervical collar	X	X	X
Spinal immobilization – long board	X	X	X
Spinal immobilization – manual	X	X	X
Spinal immobilization – seated patient (KED, etc)	X	X	X
Spinal immobilization – rapid manual extrication	X	X	X
Extremity stabilization – manual	X	X	X
Extremity splinting	X	X	X
Splint – traction	X	X	X
Mechanical patient restraint	X	X	X
Emergency moves for endangered patients	X	X	X
Skill – Medication Administration Routes	EMT	AEMT	Paramedic
Assisting a patient with his/her own prescribed medications (aerosolized/nebulized)	X	X	X
Aerosolized/nebulized (beta agonist)		X	X
Buccal		L	X
Endotracheal tube			X
Inhaled – self-administered (nitrous oxide)		X	X
Intramuscular (epinephrine or glucagon)		X	X
Intranasal (naloxone)		X	X
Inhaled – self-administered (nitrous oxide)		X	X
Intramuscular (epinephrine or glucagon)		X	X
Intranasal (naloxone)		X	X
Intravenous push (naloxone, dextrose 50%)		L	X
Intravenous piggyback			X
Nasogastric			X
Oral (glucose)	X	X	X
Oral (aspirin)	X	X	X
Rectal			X
Subcutaneous (epinephrine)		L	X
Sublingual (nitroglycerin)	X	L	X
Auto-injector (self or peer care)	X	X	X
Auto-injector (patient's own prescribed meds)	X	X	X

Revised on September 7, 2010

Skill – IV Initiation/Maintenance Fluids	EMT	AEMT	Paramedic
Access indwelling catheters and implanted central IV ports			X
Central line – monitoring			X
Intraosseous – initiation		Ped	X
Intravenous access		X	X
Intravenous initiation – peripheral		X	X
Intravenous – maintenance of non-medicated IV fluids		X	X
Intravenous – maintenance of medicated IV fluids			X
Skill – Miscellaneous	**EMT**	**AEMT**	**Paramedic**
Assisted delivery (childbirth)	X	X	X
Assisted complicated delivery (childbirth)	X	X	X
Blood glucose monitoring		X	X
Blood pressure automated	X	X	X
Blood pressure – manual	X	X	X
Eye irrigation	X	X	X
Eye irrigation – Morgan® lens			X
Thrombolytic therapy – initiation			X
Thrombolytic therapy – monitoring			X
Urinary catheterization			
Venous blood sampling			X
Blood chemistry analysis			X

Legend of Abbreviations

A	Requires additional specialty training
AI	Already Intubated
L	Limited
Ped	Pediatric Only

Revised on September 7, 2010

Appendix B

Instructions for Completing the

"NWCG Limited Request for Recognition" Form

The purpose of the *"NWCG Limited Request for Recognition"* form is to: (1) advise the state EMS authority that a Medical Unit Leader (MEDL) has established a Medical Unit within its jurisdiction, and (2) disclose all EMS personnel who are going to be rendering EMS care within that Medical Unit.

This form does not provide licensure/certification reciprocity; it only notifies state authorities of the presence of Medical Unit EMS resources. A National Registry card does not authorize EMS personnel to provide EMS patient care in any state. Only a current card issued by a state or U.S. territory EMS office will be accepted as proof of EMS license/certification.

It is the responsibility of the MEDL to complete and submit the *"NWCG Limited Request for Recognition"* form within 24 hours of the establishment of an NWCG Medical Unit. The form may be printed and filled out or filled out electronically. A new form must be completed for each incident and updated when new EMS personnel assigned to the Medical Unit arrive or move from incident to incident within that state.

To locate the state EMS authority, a "Contact List of State EMS Agencies" is provided. Contact the state EMS authority where the incident is located to determine preferred submission route for the form.

The state EMS office should acknowledge receipt of the form and validate EMS licenses of personnel providing EMS patient care. Some states have a website where this can be accomplished. If a state EMS office is unable to validate an EMS license or a license has been revoked or suspended, the MEDL should be notified.

18

NWCG LIMITED REQUEST FOR RECOGNITION

The NWCG Medical Unit Leader (MEDL) should complete this form and submit it to the state EMS authority where the Medical Unit is located. Use additional forms as necessary. MEDLs are responsible for reporting all arriving EMS personnel resources within 24 hours to the state EMS authority.

Authorization for recognition of EMS personnel is requested for the following emergency medical personnel assigned to the _____ incident (Fire Name). The identified Medical Unit personnel will provide emergency medical and health care services for incident personnel.

1.				
Full Name	License/Cert Level	State	License #	Expiration Date
2.				
Full Name	License/Cert Level	State	License #	Expiration Date
3.				
Full Name	License/Cert Level	State	License #	Expiration Date
4.				
Full Name	License/Cert Level	State	License #	Expiration Date
5.				
Full Name	License/Cert Level	State	License #	Expiration Date
6.				
Full Name	License/Cert Level	State	License #	Expiration Date

The above individual(s) will be assigned to the Medical Unit beginning _____ (Date).

The location of this NWCG incident is:

I attest that I have physically examined the state EMS license of the above individuals. (A NREMT card does not meet this requirement.)

Medical Unit Leader Name -Print	Medical Unit Leader-Signature	Date
Phone Number	Fax Number	E-Mail Address

Please indicate the preferred route of contact to the Medical Unit for communication from the state EMS office:

Phone ☐   Fax ☐   E-Mail ☐   Other

19

Revised on September 7, 2010

State EMS Office Contact List

State	State EMS Website Addresses	Phone	Fax Number
Alabama	www.adph.org	(334) 206-5383	(334) 206-5260
Alaska	www.hss.state.ak.us/dph/ipems	(907) 465-3027	(907) 465-4101
Arizona	www.azdhs.gov/bems	(602) 364-3156	(602) 364-3568
Arkansas	www.healthyarkansas.com/ems	(501) 661-2262	(501) 280-4901
California	www.emsa.ca.gov	(916) 322-4336	(916) 324-2875
Colorado	www.cdphe.state.co.us	(303) 692-2945	(303) 691-7720
Connecticut	www.dph.state.ct.us	(860) 509-7975	(860) 509-7987
Delaware	www.dhss.delaware.gov	(302) 744-5400	(302) 744-5429
District of Col.	www.bioterrorism.dc.gov	(202) 671-4222	(202) 671-0707
Florida	www.fl-ems.com	(850) 245-4053	(850) 488-9408
Georgia	www.ems.ga.gov	(404) 679-0547	(404) 679-0526
Hawaii	www.hawaii.gov/doh/resource/ems	(808) 733-9210	(808) 733-8332
Idaho	www.IdahoEMS.org	(208) 334-4000	(208) 334-4015
Illinois	www.idph.state.il.us	(217) 785-2080	(217) 524-0966
Indiana	www.in.gov/sema	(317) 232-4280	(317) 232-3895
Iowa	www.idph.state.ia.us/ems	(515) 281-0437	(515) 281-0488
Kansas	www.ksbems.org	(785) 296-7296	(785) 296-6212
Kentucky	www.kbems.ky.gov	(859) 256-3181	(859) 256-3126
Louisiana	www.dhh.louisiana.gov/offices	(225) 763-5700	(225) 763-5702
Maine	www.maine.gov/dps/ems	(207) 626-3860	(207) 287-6251
Maryland	www.miemss.org	(410) 706-5074	(410) 706-4768
Massachusetts	www.mass.gov/dph/oems	(617) 753-7300	(617) 753-7320
Michigan	www.michigan.gov/ems	(517) 241-3024	(517) 241-9458
Minnesota	www.emsrb.state.mn.us	(651) 201-2806	(651) 201-2812
Mississippi	www.msdh.state.ms.us	(601) 576-7380	(601) 576-7373
Missouri	www.dhss.mo.gov/ems	(573) 751-6356	(573) 751-6348
Montana	www.dphhs.mt.gov/ems	(406) 444-4460	(406) 444-1814
Nebraska	www.hhs.state.ne.us	(402) 471-0124	(402) 471-0169
Nevada	www.dhhs.nv.gov	(775) 687-7590	(775) 687-7595
New Hampshire	www.state.nh.us/safety/ems	(603) 223-4200	(603) 271-4567
New Jersey	www.state.nj.us/health/ems	(609) 633-7777	(609) 633-7954
New Mexico	www.nmems.org	(505) 476-8200	(505) 476-8201
New York	www.health.state.ny.us	(518) 402-0996	(518) 402-0985
North Carolina	www.ncems.org	(919) 855-3935	(919) 733-7021
North Dakota	www.ndhealth.gov/ems	(701) 328-2388	(701) 328-1890
Ohio	www.ems.ohio.gov	(614) 466-9447	(614) 995-7012
Oklahoma	www.health.state.ok.us	(405) 271-4027	(405) 271-4240
Oregon	www.dhs.state.or.us/publichealth/ems	(971) 673-1225	(971) 673-1299
Pennsylvania	www.health.state.pa.us/ems	(717) 787-8740	(717) 772-0910
Rhode Island	www.healthri.org	(401) 222-2401	(401) 222-3352
South Carolina	www.scdhec.gov	(803) 545-4275	(803) 545-4989

Revised on September 7, 2010

State	State EMS Authority Website Addresses	Phone	Fax Number
South Dakota	www.state.sd.us/dps/ems	(605) 773-3915	(605) 773-6631
Tennessee	www.state.tn.us/health	(615) 741-2584	(615) 741-4217
Texas	www.dshs.state.tx.us/emstraumasystems	(512) 834-6700	(512) 834-6736
Utah	www.health.utah.gov/ems	(801) 273-6604	(801) 273-4162
Vermont	www.state.vt.us/health/ems	(802) 863-7310	(802) 863-7577
Virginia	www.vdh.virginia.gov/oems	(804) 864-7605	(804) 864-7580
Washington	www.doh.wa.gov/hsqa/emstrauma	(360) 236-2858	(360) 236-2829
West Virginia	www.wvoems.org	(304) 558-3956	(304) 558-8379
Wisconsin	www.dhfs.wisconsin.gov/ems	(608) 261-6870	(608) 261-6392
Wyoming	www.health.wyo.gov/sho/ems	(307) 777-7955	(307) 777-5639

Appendix C
NWCG Recommended Equipment and Supply List
Emergency Medical Technician (EMT) Personnel

*Additional equipment/supplies as allowed for by licensure, credentialing and/or incident medical director and specific to incident needs. Number of items needed is dependent on the size of the incident. This list is not intended to define or limit contractual purchases.

Oxygen & Airway	
Oxygen cylinder, Jumbo-D, filled	Nasal cannula, Adult
Bag-Valve-Mask, Hand Operated, Self Re-Expanding Bag, Adult, Clear Mask, Tubing & Reservoir (no CO2)	Suction unit, hand-powered, wide-bore tubing, rigid pharyngeal curved suction tip, tonsillar, suction catheters, 5F-14F (Suction Easy, or like)
CPR Pocket Mask, "Seal Easy" Blob®, w/Oxygen Port & 2 ea one-way valve, or like	Bag, oxygen, sized to hold listed contents, & suitable for back country operations
Oxygen regulator, 0-15 LPM & 1 spare gasket	Oxygen Masks, adult, non-rebreather
Airway, Oropharyngeal (1 ea. Size 2, 3, 4, 5 & 6)	Airway, Nasopharyngeal, size 30, 32, 34 & 36 FR

Trauma Supplies	
Bandage, Gauze, Sterile, 4x4	Dressing, Finger Tip, Cloth
Bandage, Gauze, Sterile, 2x2	Dressing, Band-Aid, Cloth, 1" x 3"
Bandage, Gauze, non-sterile, 4x4 bulk	Dressing, Butterfly, Large
Bandage, Gauze, 3" x 5 yards	Dressing, Butterfly, Small
Bandage, Conforming Gauze Bandage, 4.5"	Dressing, Non-Adhering, 3" x 3", "Telfa®" or like
Bandage, Conforming Gauze Bandage, 2", or like	Dressing, Transparent, 4" x 4 1/2", "Tegaderm®" or like
Bandage, Self Adherent Wrap, Coban®, 1" or like	Dressing, Transparent, 2" x 3 1/2", "Tegaderm®" or like
Bandage, Self Adherent Wrap, Coban®, 2" or like	Bandage, underwrap, athletic
Bandage, Self Adherent Wrap, Coban®, 3" or like	Dressing, 2nd Skin®, 1" squares
Bandage, Elastic, 4", ACE® wrap or like	Dressing, 2nd Skin®, 3" circles
Tourniquet, arterial occlusion type	Dressing, 2nd Skin®, pack
Bandage, Triangular, 40" x 40" x 56"	Moleskin®, 10" x 5 yards
Dressing, Knuckle, Cloth	Dressing, Occlusive, 4" x 4" or like
Dressing, Multi-Trauma, 10" X 30"	Tape, Porous (athletic), 2"
Dressing, Combo, 5" x 9"	Tape, Transpore®, 1"
Dressing, Non-Adherent, 2" x 3"	Prep-Pad, Providone / Iodine
Tincture of Benzoin	

Revised on September 7, 2010

Equipment

Pulse Oximeter, finger w/case	Holster, belt type
Safety Pins	Shears, Bandage, 7 1/2"
Ring Cutter	Shears, Bandage, 4 1/2"
Tweezers, splinter	Shears, Trauma, 7 1/2"
Tweezers, splinter w/magnifier	Scissors, Tissue, Straight
Thermometer, Oral, digital w/10 sheath	Scissors, Tissue, Curved
Forceps, 5-1/2"	Clipper, finger nail
Sphygmomanometer, adult, of high quality	Stethoscope, of high quality
Penlight	Clipper, toe nail
Scalpel, disposable	Clipboard, 9" x 12 ½"
Magnifier, hand held, with light	Bag, Backpack first aid, "True North Medic Pack®", or like, for line walking
Automated External Defibrillator w/appropriate supporting supplies	

Splinting Items

C-Collar, Stiff Neck® Type adjustable, or like	Head Blocks, adjustable
C-Collar, Stiff Neck®, No-Neck, or like	Splint, finger
Splint, Sam® splint or like	Splint, Traction (KTD® folding or like)
Upper and lower extremity immobilization devices, air or vacuum type	Bag or case (hold listed items except backboard) w/attachment system to hold bag to backboard
Backboard, (prefer folding 350 lb. capacity)	Splints, Cardboard, assort. or like in lieu of air or vacuum
Restraint Strap(s), suggest Spider strap-color coded	Extrication Device, KED® or Oregon Spine Splint II® or like
SKED® Rescue Litter , vacuum spine board or like	Pelvic splint, T-POD®, Sam Sling® or like

Burn Supplies

Burn sheet, non-disposable	Burn sheet, disposable
Burn Kit, Water-Jel (1 ea. Dressing 36" x 30", 8" x 18", 4" x 16" & face, 3 ea. 4" x 4", 4 ea. 4" x 3" gauze a 1 ea. Scissors) or like kit	Fluid, Sodium Chloride, 0.9% (Normal Saline)

Revised on September 7, 2010

General Supplies

Pencil, mechanical or writing pen	Emergency blanket
Bag, Bio-Hazard, 5 gal, 12" x 15"	Hot pack, disposable, 5" x 8" or larger
Bag, Plastic, Zip-Lock, (snack size)	Cold pack, disposable, 5" x 8" or larger
Bag, Plastic, Zip-Lock, (gallon size)	Solution, hydrogen peroxide, 16 oz
Eye protection (full peripheral glasses or goggles)	Bedpan, disposable
Face Mask w/splash shield	Urinal, disposable
Gloves, non-latex exam, med.	Isopropyl Alcohol, 99%, cleaning
Gloves, non-latex exam, large	Betadine Solution, skin cleaning microbicide
Gloves, non-latex exam, small	Emesis bag
Gloves, non-latex exam, XL	Tongue Depressor, Sterile
Eye, Irrigating solution, 4 oz	Lock Box to store patient evaluation forms per agency regs.
Disinfectant hand wash, commercial antimicrobial (towelette, spray, liquid)	Disinfectant solution – equipment
Hand sanitizer. 4 oz	Brush, scrub surgical
Gown, disposable, open back	Syringe, Sterile, 20-60 cc (wound cleaning)
Sterile Water or Normal Saline (wound cleaning)	

Suggested Printed Items

Patient care charts/forms	OTC issue/tracking form
First Aid reference guide(s)	Medical Direction approved Protocols

* Any support supplies or items like batteries or bags to hold equipment, etc. are to be included.
** In general, equipment & supplies are to be suitable for remote field operations & fire line walking.
*** This equipment & supply list may change with updated treatment protocols & standards orders.
**** When building kits, appropriate personal protective equipment for medical personnel bloodborne pathogen and biohazard exposure is to be included.

Revised on September 7, 2010

NWCG Recommended Equipment and Supply List
Advanced EMT Personnel
(This list is in addition to the EMT equipment & supplies listed above, when medical control is established)

Airway & Equipment	
Advanced Airway kit -per medics protocols – Multi-lumen only (i.e., LMA®, King Airway, Combitube®, etc.)	Oxygen Mask, Nebulizer w/1 ea tubing, mouthpiece, tee adapter & reservoir

Equipment	
Glucometer and supplies	

IV Supplies (needleless systems required when available)	
Bag, IV starter Kit	Syringe, Sterile, assorted sizes (10, 20 & 60 cc)
IV Catheters, Protectiv® Plus, or like, assorted sizes	Tourniquet, IV, Disposable, non-latex
Pressure Infuser Bag, Disposable	Sharps case, 1 qt
IV Fluid Administration Set, Needleless, Adjustable (selec-3) Macro-drip 10-15-60 gtts	Fluid, Lactated Ringers, 1000 ml bags (per standing orders)
Syringe, Sterile, "VanishPoint®", or like, 3cc w/25g x 5/8" needle	Syringe, Sterile, "VanishPoint®", or like, 1cc w/25g x 5/8" needle
Needle, Hypodermic, 25 gauge	Needle, Hypodermic, 18 Gauge
Sharps Container, Pocket Size	Prep Pad, alcohol, large
Intraosseous device, w/supporting supplies (per standing orders)	Prep Pad, iodine/povidone, large
Fluid, Sodium Chloride, 0.9% (Normal Saline), 1000 or 500 ml. bags (or fluids per standing orders)	IV Starter kit, Veniguard® or like system

Drugs mg/ml	
Albuterol Inhaler, 17 gm, with spacer	Naloxone Hydrochloride, 2 mg per ml
Albuterol Sulfate Solution, 2.5 mg/3 ml	Nitroglycerin 0.4 mg, Tablet, 25/bottle
Dextrose 50% Injection, 25 g/50 ml	Aspirin, 325 mg, Tablet

Revised on September 7, 2010

NWCG Recommended Equipment and Supply List
Paramedic Personnel

(This list is in addition to the EMT & Advanced EMT equipment & supplies listed above, when medical control is established)

Airway & Equipment	
Advanced Airway kit - per medics protocols (i.e., ET Kit, King Airway®, etc.)	Monitor/Defibrillator, Portable, battery-operated w/appropriate supporting supplies

Drugs mg/ml	
Atropine Sulfate, 0.1 mg/1 ml, 10 ml	Epinephrine 1:10000, 0.1mg/ml, 10 ml
Adenosine, 6 mg vial	Epinephrine 1/1000, 1mg/ml, 1 ml
Sodium Bicarbonate Preload	Lidocaine 2%, 20 mg/ml, 5 ml
Diphenhydramine, 50 mg/ml, 1 ml	Lidocaine Medicated IV Drip
Magnesium Sulfate, 1 gm vial	
*Preloaded syringes preferred when available **Additional drugs as allowed for by licensure, credentialing and/or incident medical director.	

Revised on September 7, 2010

Over-the-Counter Products

This list of items is to be provided by established programs, or incident Medical Units, with medical control approval. Unit doses are preferred as available, to assure recipient retains drug identification, indications, contraindications and dosage directions.

Antacid, Tablet, unit dose	Cough Drops, Halls® type or like
Anti-Diarrheal, unit dose	Diphenhydramine, 25 mg caps or dissolving strips, unit dose
Anti-Fungal Cream, Athlete's Foot, .5 oz, unit dose	Hand Lotion, unit dose
Anti-Itch Cream, Hydrocortisone 1%, 1/32oz, unit dose	Eye drops, 1/2, unit dose
Anti-Pain gel or liquid , Tooth, unit dose	Eye Irrigating Solution, 4 oz
Nasal Spray, saline, unit dose	Lip Balm, unit dose SPF (Hydrating not wax)
Anti-Pain/Inflammatory, Acetaminophen, 500 mg, unit dose	Bacitracin® Ointment, or Polysporin®, or like, 1/32 oz, unit dose
Anti-Pain/Inflammatory, Aspirin, 325 mg, unit dose	Nasal Decongestant, "Afrin Spray®", unit dose
Anti-Pain/Inflammatory, Ibuprofen, 200 mg, unit dose	Nasal Decongestant, Day Time, unit dose
Anti-Pain/Inflammatory, Naproxen, 220 mg, unit dose	Nasal Decongestant, Night Time, unit dose
Muscle Rub, Ben Gay® or like, 2 oz	Providone-Iodine, ampoules
Bag Balm®/Aquaphor®, unit dose	Glucose, Insta 15g, unit dose
Cough Drop, Chloraseptic®, or like, unit dose	Tampon & Sanitary Napkins
Foot Powder, 2 to 4 oz., Gold Bond® or like	Anti-Itch Cream, Calagel® or like, unit dose
Poison ivy/oak creams – Tecnu®, Zanfe®l or like	Lotion, Sun Block, 20 SPF or higher, 1 to 2 oz.
Hemorrhoidal suppositories or creams	Dextrose, tube, 15gm
Cough suppressant, mucolytic or like	Acid Reducer (Prilosec®, Zantac®, Tagamet®)

Revised on September 7, 2010